Martin Luthe

Rob Lloyd Jones

Designed by Leonard Le Rolland

History consultant: David James

Reading consultant: Alison Kelly, Roehampton University

SCHOLASTIC INC.

New York   Toronto   London   Auckland   Sydney
Mexico City   New Delhi   Hong Kong   Buenos Aires

ISBN-13: 978-0-439-02299-6
ISBN-10: 0-439-02299-1

12 11 10 9 8 7 6 5 4 3   7 8 9 10 11 12/0

Printed in the U.S.A.   23

First Scholastic printing, January 2007

Edited by Jane Chisholm

American editor Carrie Armstrong

Digital imaging by Leonard Le Rolland

Cover design by Russell Punter

Acknowledgements:

© Corbis cover (Bettmann), p1 (Flip Schulke), pp2-3 (E.O. Hoppé), p5 (Flip Schulke), p7 (Bettmann), p8 (Flip Schulke), pp14-15 (Bettmann), p16, p19 (Flip Schulke), p20 (John Van Hasselt/Corbis Sygma), p21 and p22 (Bettmann), p25 (Flip Schulke), p26 and p27 (Bettmann), p28 (Flip Schulke), pp30-31, p35, p36, p39 and p40 (Bettmann), p42 (Flip Schulke), pp44-45 (Bettmann), pp46-47 (Flip Schulke), p49 and p51 (Bettmann), pp52-53 (Flip Schulke), p54 to pp64-65 (Bettmann), back cover (Flip Schulke); © Getty Images pp10-11, p13, p17 (Time Life Pictures/Getty Images), p32 (Time Life Pictures/Getty Images), p37 (Time Life Pictures/Getty Images); © Magnum PI p43 (Bob Adelamn), p55 (Eli Reed).

Every effort has been made to trace and acknowledge ownership of copyright. The publishers offer to rectify any omissions in future editions, following notification.

Contents

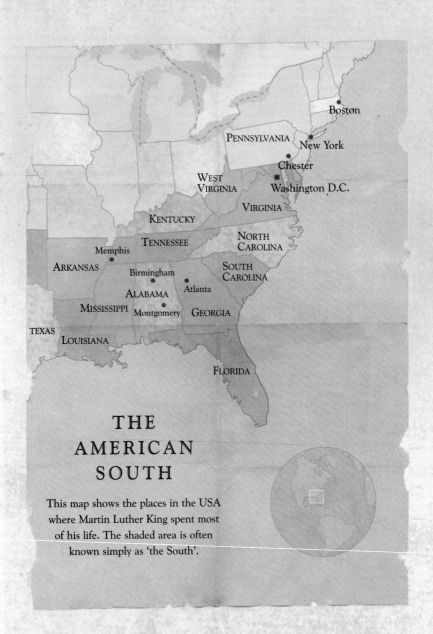

Boston

PENNSYLVANIA
New York

Chester

WEST
VIRGINIA
Washington D.C.

VIRGINIA

KENTUCKY

TENNESSEE
NORTH
CAROLINA

Memphis

ARKANSAS
Birmingham
SOUTH
CAROLINA

ALABAMA
Atlanta

MISSISSIPPI
Montgomery
GEORGIA

TEXAS
LOUISIANA

FLORIDA

THE
AMERICAN
SOUTH

This map shows the places in the USA
where Martin Luther King spent most
of his life. The shaded area is often
known simply as 'the South'.

Ebenezer Baptist Church in Atlanta, Georgia, where Martin Luther King Jr.'s father worked as a minister.

Chapter 1

Proud parents

The bells of Ebenezer Baptist Church rang out in Atlanta, Georgia, on the morning of January 15, 1929. Inside, a crowd of smiling faces gathered to congratulate Reverend King and his wife Alberta on the birth of their first son.

But as the happy parents shook hands with the congregation, they felt a mix of emotions. Like all black people in the southern states of the USA, the Kings lived under the ugly shadow of segregation – a series of laws that kept black people apart from whites and made them feel like second-class citizens. They loved their son, but they were sad that he had been born into a society that would treat him so unfairly.

In towns and cities across the South, black people – or *Negroes* as they were called then – were forced to drink from separate fountains, attend separate schools and play in separate parks. They were banned from certain restaurants, made to stand up on buses and even had to step into the gutter when white people passed them on the street.

The Kings had tried to fight for their right to be treated as equals. Like many other black Americans, they had organized protest marches and given speeches in church. But it had made no difference. America remained divided.

So, as they watched their son sleep that night, the Kings offered a desperate prayer. They prayed he would grow up in a better society. They prayed he would live to see change.

Black people across the South had to drink water from different faucets than whites. These had signs on them reading 'colored'.

WHITE MEN COLORED MEN

COLORED

This is 501 Auburn Avenue in Atlanta, Georgia – the house where Martin Luther King grew up.

Chapter 2

Loss of innocence

Six years later, young Martin Luther King was hiding at the top of the stairs with his little brother Alfred. They needed to think fast. Their piano teacher would be here any minute and they both hated her lessons.

"I've got it!" Alfred announced. "We can sneak down and smash up the piano."

Martin considered Alfred's plan, but shook his head. He had a better idea.

Half an hour later, Martin's mother gathered the pair in the lounge for their lesson. But, as she greeted the piano teacher, there were two things she failed to notice. The first was the grins on her sons' faces, and the second was that the piano stool's legs had been loosened...

As the teacher sat down, the stool collapsed, sending her and her music flying backwards.

"Martin! Alfred!" Mrs. King screamed. But the boys had already darted out of the door.

Martin ran down the street to his best friend's house. He loved Atlanta on summer evenings, especially the way the sun set across the old wooden houses. But summer was almost over and soon school would start. He was determined to have as much fun as possible first.

Martin darted up to his friend's house and jumped to ring the doorbell. After a second, his friend's father answered. The tall man looked at Martin, then closed the door a little. "My son can't come out," he said. "You two can't play together anymore."

Martin was startled. "Why not?" he asked.
The man stared down at him, his eyes
suddenly cold and serious. "Because you're
black and he's white," he said, and then he
slammed the door.

Later that day, Martin asked his mother
what the man had meant. She looked sad for
a moment, then, very carefully, she explained.
She told her son about the history of black
people in America – how they had once been
slaves but were now free, and many white
people couldn't accept that.

This photo shows white children playing in
Atlanta's streets in the 1940s. Many of their
parents refused to allow black children like
Martin Luther King to join in.

Then Martin's mother looked deep into his eyes. Martin had never seen her so serious. "No matter what the rest of the world says," she told him, "you're as good as anyone else."

In a way, Martin lost his innocence that day. Until then, he'd never noticed the differences between the way black and white people lived, but now he saw them everywhere. He saw assistants in shops serving black people last. In the streets, he saw white people watching him with fear and suspicion. Suddenly it was as if Atlanta was two different worlds – one for white people and one for blacks.

Martin still played around and got into trouble like any other boy, but there was a fire inside him now which would never go out. From that day on, he was determined to prove his mother right and show the whole world that he was as good as anyone else.

He began to study harder at school, spending more and more time reading books and writing essays. By the time he was fourteen, he was getting the best grades in his class. He even won a local speech competition. Martin's parents were so proud – not only because he had worked hard, but also because of the subject he chose for his speech: the history of black people in America.

A white shopkeeper stands by a sign banning black people from entering his store. This is the sort of scene Martin Luther King saw in the streets of Atlanta every day.

On the bus home from the competition, Martin and his teacher were so excited that they barely heard the voice booming down on them.

"Get up!"

An angry white man was standing over their seat. The rest of the bus was now full and he didn't want to stand. "Get up!" he repeated. "Negroes should stand."

Martin's teacher stood up, but Martin didn't move. The bus stopped and the driver rushed down the aisle.

"Give the man your seat," he shouted to Martin. "Negroes have to stand."

The white man and the driver swore at Martin, but still he refused to move. Then Martin's teacher put a gentle hand on his shoulder and smiled at him. "It's the law, Martin," she said quietly.

Martin didn't want his teacher to get into trouble, so he finally gave up his seat. As he stood in the cramped aisle, a mix of emotions

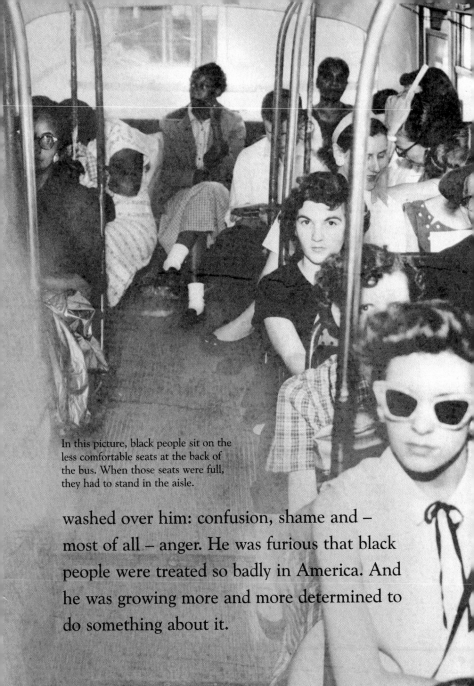

In this picture, black people sit on the less comfortable seats at the back of the bus. When those seats were full, they had to stand in the aisle.

washed over him: confusion, shame and – most of all – anger. He was furious that black people were treated so badly in America. And he was growing more and more determined to do something about it.

Chapter 3

A serious student

In 1944, Martin enrolled at Morehouse College in Atlanta, a school for black students that his father had also attended. Morehouse was an exciting place for fifteen-year-old Martin. He quickly made new friends around the tree-lined campus, attending dances and playing on the school football team. But inside he was still confused, not only about the society he lived in, but the life he wanted to live. Martin wanted to help change things in the South, but he didn't know how.

At first, he thought he might become a lawyer and fight for equality for black people (known as their 'civil rights') through the courts. But the more he read, the more interested he became in religion. It was church ministers like his father that the black community looked to for guidance and support.

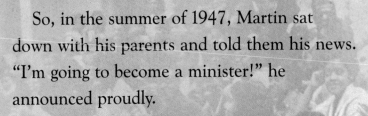

So, in the summer of 1947, Martin sat down with his parents and told them his news. "I'm going to become a minister!" he announced proudly.

Here, students enjoy a lecture at Morehouse College, the school Martin Luther King Jr. attended between 1944 and 1948.

Martin's father was pleased his son wanted to become a church leader like him, but he was cautious too. Not everyone had the skills needed to lead church services. He decided Martin should preach a trial sermon at his church in Atlanta.

On the morning he was due to preach, it was difficult to tell who was more nervous, Martin or his father. But neither of them needed to worry. From the moment Martin took the stage, the power and passion of his words gripped the entire congregation. That night, Martin's father thanked God for blessing him with such a son.

Martin now decided he wanted to study at Crozer Seminary, a school for church ministers in Chester, Pennsylvania. Crozer was an excellent college but, more importantly, it was a long way north of Atlanta. It offered Martin his first chance to experience the world beyond the deep South.

Martin Luther King delivers a sermon from the pulpit of his father's church in Atlanta, Georgia.

19

Martin Luther King (circled) listens to a lecture at Crozer.

Martin enjoyed life at Crozer. The northern states of the USA were less racist than the South, so black and white students at the college studied together. It was a great opportunity for Martin – a chance to prove that a black student could achieve as much as anybody else. He studied harder than ever, earning high grades in all his subjects. He even began to dress in a way he thought made him look more serious, attending lectures every day in the same immaculate brown suit and shoes.

For the first time, Martin began thinking seriously about how he could help fight racism in the South. Some black students suggested rioting, but Martin hated the idea of violence.

Towards the end of his time at Crozer, he attended a lecture about Mahatma Gandhi, a famous civil rights leader who had fought for independence in India. As Martin listened, he grew more and more fascinated. Gandhi had been a small, quiet man, but he had changed the future of a whole nation – not through war or violence, but through peaceful protest and dogged determination. To Martin, Gandhi was everything a leader should be. He hoped that one day black Americans would have one as great.

This is a photograph of Mahatma Gandhi, the famous Indian civil rights leader. Gandhi died in 1948, the year that Martin Luther King began his studies at Crozer.

A picture of Martin Luther King with
his wife Coretta Scott. They met at the
University of Boston in February 1952.

22

Chapter 4

Young love

Martin's hard work at Crozer paid off. He graduated at the top of his class, and was offered a scholarship to the university of his choice. He decided to go further north and study theology at the University of Boston.

Settled in Boston, Martin began to relax and enjoy his final year of education. But he also missed home. To cheer him up, Martin's friends suggested he meet another black student from the South, a young woman named Coretta Scott.

Martin and Coretta met on a rainy day in a little Boston café. They liked each other immediately and stayed talking until the evening. They discussed college, the arts and dancing. But, most of all, they talked about the South.

The pair met regularly throughout that spring and summer at Boston. They studied together, attended concerts and went dancing. But mostly they just walked and talked about whatever came to mind. One day, when they were out walking, Martin took Coretta firmly by the hand.

"You have everything I want in a woman," he told her, "character, intelligence, personality and beauty. Will you marry me?"

Coretta hesitated. She did love Martin, and wanted to marry him, but she also knew what it meant. By now Martin was a fully qualified minister and he'd recently been offered a job as a preacher in Montgomery, a town in the South. Coretta wasn't sure she could return to a place that had caused her so much pain. As a child growing up in Alabama, she had seen her father being attacked by white thugs. The memory still haunted her.

"Couldn't we stay here," she said, "where things are not so tough?"

This picture, taken in the southern state of Alabama, shows how strongly some white people felt about keeping blacks separate.

Martin let go of Coretta's hand. He knew they could build a comfortable life together in Boston. But he also knew he couldn't stay. He stared deep into Coretta's eyes, hoping she would understand.

"I have to go back to the South," Martin said softly. "It's where I'm needed."

By now Coretta knew Martin better than anyone, so she recognized the look in his eyes. She took his hand and smiled. "Then I will come with you," she said. "As your wife."

Martin and Coretta traveled south to be married in Alabama on a perfect summer's day in June 1953. Martin's father conducted the ceremony and both families watched as the young couple climbed into their car and set off for their new life in Montgomery. As they drove away, Martin saw a bus go by. All the white people inside were seated and all the black people were standing. He knew he had made the right decision to return.

This photograph, taken in 1956, shows Martin Luther and Coretta Scott King in the first happy years of their marriage.

Here, Rosa Parks is seen sitting in a 'Whites Only' section of a Montgomery bus.

Chapter 5

A leader is born

On December 1, 1955, Martin Luther King received a phone call from his friend, E.D. Nixon. "Have you heard about Rosa Parks?" E.D. asked excitedly. Martin didn't recognize the name, so E.D. explained.

Earlier that evening, a black woman named Rosa Parks had left work at a Montgomery department store and boarded a bus home. Tired from a long day, Rosa was relieved to find an empty seat behind the 'Whites Only' section.

As the bus filled, the driver ordered her to give the seat up for a white passenger. Like Martin had done years before, Rosa refused. But, unlike Martin, Rosa was arrested.

"This is the opportunity we've been waiting for," said E.D. Martin knew right away what he meant. He had been living in Montgomery for a year now and the two men often spoke about segregation. They both wanted to do something to bring about changes. Now Rosa's arrest had given E.D. an idea.

Martin Luther King spoke to hundreds of black people in Montgomery, encouraging them to take part in the bus boycott on December 5, 1955.

"We'll boycott the buses for a day in protest," he suggested.

The plan appealed to Martin – it reminded him of Gandhi's non-violent protests in India. Even so, no one had ever attempted anything like it in Montgomery and it would take a huge amount of planning. Martin and Coretta had recently had their first child, a daughter named Yolanda. Now, more than ever, Martin felt he was needed at home. That night, he spoke to Coretta about E.D.'s plan. "I'm not sure how much time I'd have at home," he said. "This boycott would mean a lot of work."

Coretta listened, then she smiled. "Then you'd better get busy."

Martin got very busy, just like others in the black community. Soon they were printing leaflets and making calls, letting thousands of black people who used Montgomery's buses know about the boycott. "Don't ride the buses on Monday," they urged everyone. "We're fighting for our freedom."

That Monday, Martin woke at dawn. He paced around his house, trying to hide his nerves. He had no idea if the boycott would work. What if no one took part? Then he heard Coretta shout from the kitchen.

"Martin! Look outside!"

Martin rushed to the window. The morning bus was passing his house – and it was empty! Hundreds of black people filled the streets. Some were walking, some were cycling, one was even riding a mule – but no one was using the bus. Martin grinned from ear to ear. The boycott seemed to be working.

Protesters in Montgomery wave at an empty bus after the start of the boycott in December 1955.

Martin rushed to his church on Dexter Avenue to meet the other protest leaders. Everyone was excited, shouting at once.

"This could last even longer," someone said. "We'll force the bus company to change its policy," another person shouted. "But who's going to lead us?" Suddenly they all turned and looked at Martin.

Martin was stunned. He was proud to be associated with the boycott, but he had never expected to lead it.

"Well, if you think I can," he said proudly, "then I will."

Martin took his new position seriously. He organized groups of cars to drive people to work and each night he gave speeches in his church, encouraging everyone to continue the boycott. Montgomery's buses remained empty for weeks, then months. People walked through the cold winter rain, then the hot summer sun. They walked for freedom.

But the city officials refused to back down. Instead of changing the seating policy on the

A bus sits empty in the background as protesters in Montgomery travel by car instead. Martin Luther King helped organize dozens of carpools like this to carry protesters to work.

buses, they searched for a way to stop the boycott. When they couldn't find one, they turned against its leader. One morning, as Martin was leading a protest meeting, his friend Ralph Abernathy burst through the doors.

"Martin," he gasped, "your house… it's been bombed!"

Martin drove home as fast as he could. As he arrived, he saw smoke rising from the front of his house. His heart pounded with fear. But then he saw them – Coretta and Yolanda – they were safe. Wrapping his arms around them, Martin cried with relief.

The black community was outraged. Within minutes, dozens of them had gathered at the bomb site. Some carried knives, others held guns – everyone was ready to fight if Martin gave the word. But what happened next amazed them all. Letting go of his family, Martin climbed onto the smoldering remains of his porch and looked down at the crowd.

"Love," he shouted, "I want you to love our enemies. We can't let their hate stop us."

No one could believe it. Martin's house had just been bombed, his family almost killed, but still he was calling for peace. The crowd stared at him with admiration and amazement. And, in that moment, they realized they had a true leader at last.

From that night on, Martin doubled his efforts on behalf of the boycott, touring the city and encouraging the protesters with his powerful speeches.

"If you have found a correct course," he told them, "you do not retreat – you struggle to win a victory."

The city officials increased their efforts too, threatening Martin in private and spreading lies about him in the newspapers. They even tried to stop the protesters from carpooling, so they would have to use the buses. But Martin and the black community refused to break – and the buses stayed empty.

Shortly after the bombing of his own house, Martin Luther King stood on his front porch and called for peace.

Then, as Martin was with the boycott leaders one morning, someone handed him a telegram. It was from the US Supreme Court, the highest court in the nation. Martin opened it and read what they had to say. Then he read it again.

"Well?" someone finally asked.

Martin looked up, dazed. "The Supreme Court has decided that segregation on buses is illegal," he said. It was all he could do to whisper the next words: "We've won."

On December 21, 1956, Martin boarded his first bus in over a year. He nodded hello to the driver, then took his seat – directly beneath the 'Whites Only' sign.

It was the best ride of his life.

Martin Luther King (wearing the hat) travels on a Montgomery bus in December 1956, shortly after the Supreme Court declared segregation on buses illegal.

Martin Luther King appeared on the cover
of this popular magazine in February 1957.

Chapter 6

The struggle continues

Things began to happen fast after the
boycott. News of the protesters' success
spread quickly across the country. Suddenly
every black American wanted to hear more
from the man whose courage had led the
protesters to victory.

Martin hadn't set out to be a leader. But, now that he'd become one, he never missed an opportunity to campaign against segregation. He wrote a book about the bus boycott named *Stride Toward Freedom*, and in 1957 he agreed to become chairman of the Southern Christian Leadership Conference (SCLC), a group of senior black ministers who promoted civil rights. The position was based in Atlanta, so Martin waved a sad farewell to Montgomery and returned with Coretta and Yolanda to his old hometown.

Martin's parents were delighted, welcoming him back in church with huge smiles. "He is not little Martin anymore," his father told the congregation, "he is *Dr. King* now."

Martin's parents were right to be proud. Their son's courage had inspired black people across America to take action of their own. In Arkansas, black students marched through racist mobs to attend newly integrated schools. In North Carolina, several protesters sat at

'Whites Only' lunch counters – refusing to leave until they were either served or arrested. Soon, these 'sit-ins' had spread all over the South. By the time they reached Atlanta, Martin was ready to join them.

A black student sits at a lunch counter in Nashville, Tennessee, in protest against unfair segregation laws. Bundles of napkins have been placed next to him to discourage others from joining in.

On October 19, 1960, Martin walked into a department store in the middle of Atlanta and sat with several other protesters at a 'Whites Only' lunch counter. He was arrested within minutes, but it didn't matter. TV cameras had broadcast his protest to the whole nation. His message was clear – he was happy to go to jail in the name of freedom.

After a week in a dank jail cell, Martin emerged exhausted. Since Montgomery, he had traveled thousands of miles and given his support to dozens of protests. He was happy at last to have some time at home with his family. By 1963, he and Coretta had three more children, boys named Martin Luther and Dexter Scott, and a girl named Bernice Albertine. Martin relished every minute with them and Yolanda – reading together, playing baseball, or just sitting in the yard staring at the clouds. But, even at home, they couldn't escape the shadow of segregation.

Police lead Martin Luther King from a protest in downtown Atlanta. Even as he was taken to jail, Martin vowed to continue to fight segregation.

One evening, Martin was sitting with Yolanda when an advertisement for a local fair came on the television. Yolanda's eyes lit up immediately.

"Can we go, Daddy?" she pleaded.

Martin's heart sank. Yolanda was six now, and growing smarter every day. But there were a lot of things she didn't understand yet. She didn't realize that the fair wasn't open to black children.

Martin Luther King and his daughter Yolanda sit on a swing at their home in Atlanta.

That night, Martin lay awake thinking about the past few years. Protests such as sit-ins had brought an end to segregation in hundreds of towns across the South, but black people remained second-class citizens. The time had come to make a bigger statement.

A sign welcoming people to the city of Birmingham, Alabama, where Martin Luther King led a civil rights campaign in 1963.

Chapter 7

Battle for Birmingham

Dark clouds rumbled over downtown Atlanta as Martin Luther King entered the SCLC headquarters on Auburn Avenue. He was now working as a minister at his father's Baptist church, but he also met regularly with the SCLC to discuss the civil rights movement in the South.

"We need to start a new campaign," Martin said as the group sat around the meeting table.

Martin's friend Ralph Abernathy sat up, sipping his coffee. "Whereabouts?" he asked.

"Birmingham," replied Martin quickly.

Ralph almost choked. "You're crazy!" he spluttered. "Birmingham's the most segregated city in the South!"

Martin smiled at his friend mischievously. "Exactly," he replied.

Suddenly everyone in the room understood. The industrial city of Birmingham was in the heart of Alabama, a state famous for its governor's promise of "Segregation today, segregation tomorrow, segregation forever!" If their campaign could succeed there, it could succeed anywhere.

So, in April 1963 Martin and the SCLC wrote a list of their demands for change in Birmingham. They only had two: fair treatment and fair pay for black people. Birmingham's government responded quickly with their comments. They only had one: Never. The battle was on.

Preparations began immediately. Martin flew to Birmingham and met his old friend Fred

Shuttleworth. Together, they toured the city's steel factories, pool halls and churches, encouraging everyone they met to join in the protest. "Freedom!" they shouted. "Bring freedom to Birmingham!"

This photograph, taken in 1965, shows Martin Luther King giving one of his powerful speeches to a crowd of young supporters.

The campaign began with sit-ins. Suddenly, restaurants and department stores across the city were flooded with protesters demanding equal rights for the city's black population.

The police reacted immediately. Led by their racist chief Eugene 'Bull' Connor, they dragged the protesters into vans and threw them into jail cells. The SCLC quickly bailed them out, but soon their bail money had run dry. Now, anyone sent to jail risked staying there.

Alone in his motel, Martin said a prayer. "We're struggling not to save ourselves," he prayed, "but to save the soul of this nation. Give us strength."

Lines of white policemen blocked the streets
of Birmingham, Alabama in May 1963.

That morning, he left his usual brown suit
behind and put on his old blue overalls instead.
Martin was going to work.

As the sun rose on Good Friday 1963, he led
dozens of supporters in a march to Birmingham
City Hall. More and more people rushed to the
roadside as they passed. Some climbed on
rooftops, cheering and waving in support.
Martin had never felt so determined, or so
proud of the people he walked with.

Then, as they reached the city center, he
stopped. Hundreds of policemen were blocking
the road ahead.

"Bull Connor says go home, boy," one of them shouted. "Blacks ain't welcome here."

The marchers waited nervously, unsure what Martin would do next. Then, very quietly, Martin knelt down on the hot tarmac and began to pray. After a second, every other protester did the same.

The police didn't hesitate. Martin and the other protesters were dragged from the streets, but none of them fought back. Police dogs tore at their arms, but none of them fought back. One by one they were thrown into cells without beds or windows. But, even then, none of them fought back. They refused to let their spirits break.

Locked in a dirty cell, Martin managed to get hold of a pen. He wrote a letter to the people of Birmingham.

"One has a moral responsibility," he told them, "to disobey unjust laws... Oppressed people cannot remain oppressed forever."

Martin's 'Letter from Birmingham Jail' –
written on scraps of newspaper – was smuggled
from his cell. Almost a million copies were
circulated around the United States.

Locked in jail in April 1963,
Martin Luther King considers
the next stage of the campaign
in Birmingham, Alabama.

By the time Martin was released a few days later, thousands more volunteers were ready to join the fight. But these new protesters were different. Just like the previous marchers, they were brave and determined. But, unlike the others, they were children. On May 2, 1963, over a thousand schoolboys and girls held hands and sang joyful songs of freedom as they marched into Birmingham. But their voices soon grew faint. Several fire trucks blocked their path. Bull Connor stood beside them, his teeth gritted in anger.

"Let 'em have it!" he yelled.

Suddenly, dozens of firemen stepped forward carrying high-pressure hoses. Massive jets of water blasted into the young marchers, smashing them apart like bowling pins. Some were tossed into the air, others slammed against walls. Before they could recover, the police were on them, grabbing as many as possible. Those who weren't arrested ran away.

But the next day they came again. This time

Bull Connor got tougher. The marchers were hammered with batons, savaged by dogs and even beaten with iron rods. The shocking images were broadcast on television screens across America. Millions watched in horror as black men, women and children were battered and abused simply for their right to be treated as equal citizens.

Terrified young protesters flee from Birmingham police in May 1963.

Then, on the fourth day, something amazing happened. As the protesters marched into the town center, Bull Connor yelled for the firemen to turn on their hoses. But this time they refused. He shouted the order again, but the firemen stood firm.

Martin knew what it meant: Birmingham had had enough. Its streets were awash with the blood of beaten protesters. Shops and businesses were boarded up. Jails were overcrowded, and hospitals were filled with broken and bruised marchers. The city could take no more.

In May 1963, Birmingham City Hall made an announcement. From now on, black people could eat where they wished, sit where they wished and walk where they wished. When Martin heard the news, he cried with joy.

But, even now, he had one more march to make.

On August 28, 1963, Martin led 250,000 euphoric supporters to the nation's capital, Washington D.C. This time the crowds weren't just black – by now the whole country cared about civil rights.

Encouraged by Martin Luther King, black and white protesters march together to Washington D.C. on August 28, 1963.

Martin Luther King gave his famous "I have a dream" speech in Washington D.C. on August 28, 1963.

They came together beneath the blazing sun to hear Martin Luther King deliver one of the greatest speeches in American history. Standing in the shadow of the Lincoln memorial, he told them about a dream he had.

"I have a dream," he said, "that one day on the red hills of Georgia the sons of former slaves and the sons of former slave owners will be able to sit down together at the table of brotherhood... I have a dream that my four children will one day live in a nation where they will not be judged by the color of their skin but by the content of their character."

Martin's voice roared from the stage, growing louder and stronger with each word.

"And when we let freedom ring," he continued, "when we let it ring from every village and every hamlet, from every state and every city, we will be able to speed up that day when all of God's children, black men and white men, Jews and Gentiles, Protestants and Catholics, will be able to join hands and sing... Free at last! Free at last! Thank God Almighty, we are free at last!"

250,000 protesters gathered in Washington D.C. to hear Martin's incredible speech on August 28, 1963.

Chapter 8
Triumph and tragedy

Martin Luther King's Washington speech was greeted with mixed reactions. While most of America celebrated, those who still supported segregation grew even more hateful. Back in Birmingham, a group of racists hurled a bomb into a packed church. As the dust settled, the bodies of four black choirgirls lay among the ruins.

In December 1964, Martin traveled to Norway to be awarded the Nobel Peace Prize. It was a huge honor, but after the bombing it felt meaningless. What future did peace have in the face of such violence?

Even so, Martin refused to give up. He now turned his attention to voting rights for black people, organizing a campaign in Selma, Alabama, and then leading a fifty-mile march to Montgomery.

The marchers were rained on, taunted, even pelted with rocks, but once again they won. In August 1965, President Lyndon B. Johnson signed an act removing restrictions on black voting rights. Now that black Americans had the power to vote, politicians and city officials would have to treat them very differently.

Martin Luther and Coretta Scott King lead a protest march from Selma, Alabama, on March 21, 1965.

Even so, Martin couldn't shake his depression. In the ten years since the Montgomery bus boycott, segregation had been hugely reduced in the South. But a new generation of black Americans were growing up with a new set of problems. Their pay was lower than white people's and their living conditions much worse. Faced with such inequality, many questioned the value of peaceful protests. Instead of 'freedom', they shouted 'power'. Instead of marching, they rioted. In the summer of 1965, hundreds of black youths clashed with police in Los Angeles, California, trashing shops and burning cars in the city streets.

Martin was desperate to remind the country how much non-violent action could achieve. In the spring of 1968, he and Ralph Abernathy traveled to Memphis, Tennessee, to lead a march in support of black workers.

At first, the protest went well. But as it entered the city's shopping district, things turned ugly. One protester pushed a policeman, and another threw a brick into a shop window. Martin shouted for calm, but it was too late – the march was in chaos. Police charged at the youths and, as the crowd fought back, Martin and Ralph ran for their lives.

Back in his motel, Martin watched the riots on the news. The pictures made him feel sick. Peaceful protest had achieved so much, but it seemed that many black people now thought violence was the answer to their problems. Martin wanted nothing to do with it. He stared at the rain pouring outside his window, wishing he was back home with Coretta and his children.

Suddenly, the phone rang. It was Ralph.

Fires rage in the streets of Los Angeles, California, as civil rights protests turn violent in August 1965.

"The protest leaders are gathered in a church downtown," he said desperately. "Maybe you can talk to them."

Martin was tired, but he had to try. Ten minutes later, he arrived at the church soaked with rain. On the way over, he had planned what he might say, but as he stood above the crowds, the words just came from his heart. He told them about the miracle that had happened in Montgomery. He told them about the pride of the marchers in Birmingham. He told them about Atlanta, Selma, and every other town where courage and determination had won black people their freedom.

The power and passion of Martin's words gripped everyone in the church, drowning out the storm that raged outside. When he finished, everyone agreed they would march by his side. And they would march peacefully.

Martin beamed with a joy unlike any he'd known. For the first time, he felt that this new generation might face their troubles with the

Martin Luther King appeals to the youth of Memphis on April 3, 1968. This was to be his last ever speech.

same dignity that thousands of black Americans had in the past. The future was in their hands.

"We've got some difficult days ahead," he told them. "But it doesn't matter with me now. Because I've been to the mountaintop... And I've looked over. And I've seen the Promised Land."

The next day – April 4, 1968 – Martin met Ralph Abernathy at his motel and began planning a new march. He was still tired, but as he stepped onto his balcony and breathed the spring air, he felt a new strength for the future.

"Tomorrow's going to be a great day," he shouted to Ralph.

Inside his room, Ralph laughed. Then he heard a gunshot. He rushed outside and found his friend lying on the hotel balcony – struck down by an assassin's bullet.

An hour later, Martin Luther King died at St. Joseph's Hospital in Memphis. His killer, a racist named James Earl Ray, was caught soon after.

Five days later, the bells rang out again at Ebenezer Baptist Church in Atlanta, Georgia. Thousands of mourners gathered for their final march with Martin, carrying his coffin past Morehouse College and on to South View Cemetery.

Then they all said goodbye to the man who had proved to the world that he was as good as anyone else.

Huge crowds gather in Atlanta, Georgia, for the funeral of Martin Luther King on April 9, 1968. Martin's coffin was carried on an old-fashioned mule cart, symbolizing the struggle against poverty and hardship faced by millions of black people across America.